Tracy, Stacy, Marcy, and Tommy

by Nancy Tyler
illustrated by Robert Casilla

Practice Decodable 6I

McGraw Hill Education

Bothell, WA • Chicago, IL • Columbus, OH • New York, NY

MHEonline.com

Send all inquiries to:
McGraw-Hill Education
8787 Orion Place
Columbus, OH 43240

ISBN: 978-0-02-132784-3
MHID: 0-02-132784-X

Printed in China.

8 9 10 11 12 DSS 27 26 25 24 23

Tommy had three sisters.
Tracy, Stacy, and Marcy liked winter.

"I like to skate on ponds," said Tracy.
"I can do some fancy tricks."

Stacy liked to study pretty flakes.
"Each flake looks lacy," she said.

"Winter is fun here," said Marcy.
"I like to race down icy hills."

"I do not like winter," said Tommy.
"I will just make hot, spicy cider."

"This cider is tasty," said his sisters.
"Could we have some more?"